Advanced Praise

Leduc's poetry—his work--ain't strip-mined, but is rooted in earth, hearth, and heart. In *Slagflower*, the poet retrieves true grit, the honest nugget (no fool's gold), and diamonds that are truly squeezed out of coal. Leduc is so skilled at heavy lifting, his touch is deft. You almost don't notice the toil--the hard work of making--that's produced this art, this sculpted masterpiece.
– George Elliott Clarke, 7th Parliamentary Poet Laureate (2016 & 2017)

Plain-spoken yet beautifully crafted, these poems resound with deep history and authentic feeling. Gripping – I read them in one sitting.
– Susan McMaster, poet and editor

Tom Leduc's work reflects Sudbury's origins, a unique series of mining poems that speak openly "of sulphur and ash, of man and metal." Leduc fashions a definitive sense of place, creates characters who are people we've all known and loved, and uses a warm, narrative voice to draw readers in.
– Kim Fahner, *These Wings* (Pedlar Press), Poet Laureate of Greater Sudbury (2016-18)

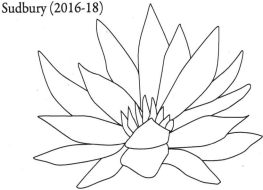

The production of this book was made possible through the generous assistance
of the Ontario Arts Council.

ONTARIO ARTS COUNCIL
CONSEIL DES ARTS DE L'ONTARIO
an Ontario government agency
un organisme du gouvernement de l'Ontario

Library and Archives Canada Cataloguing in Publication

Leduc, Thomas 1966-, author
Slagflower / Thoams Leduc.

ISBN 978-1-988989-10-5 (softcover)

I. Title.

PS8611.A765W38 2018   C813'.6   C2018-902063-6

Printed and bound in Canada on 100% recycled paper.

Book design: Maurissa Zuccolo
Cover Art: Thomas Leduc
Author photo: Marg Seregyli

Published by:
Latitude 46 Publishing
info@latitude46publishing.com
Latitude46publishing.com

Slagflower
Poems Unearthed
From A Mining Town

By Thomas Leduc

LATITUDE 46
PUBLISHING

For my father Louis Leduc and his father Guy Leduc
and his father Olivier Leduc
and all the fathers and grandfathers and aunts, uncles,
cousins, brothers and everyone who ever worked in a mine.
Thank you for getting us to this place.

Contents

Section V: Slagflower

Section I
Birthmark

Birthmark

What I remember most
was the emptiness
nothing but black rock
and blue sky welded together
like the brushstrokes
of a Dali painting.
Surreal, disproportioned
and out of place.

I liked the way this oddity
stood out shiny and oversized
pushed to the outskirts of town
reflecting how I felt
on the edge of manhood.

My long hair, and brown
bell bottom cords
flapping in the wind
drumming out my future.
My eyes squinting
my mouth an open hole.
My hand struggling
to block the screaming glare.

I was an ant
in a desert of black rock
looking up at a silver flower.
A birthmark on the back
of a mining town.

The damn thing looked
as if it was a gift
from the god Pluto
like a piece of change
had slipped out of his fingers
rose through the cracks
of the earth and surfaced in
my backyard.

A Big Nickel
to pay the ferryman
and reveal to me
a way out of this underworld.

Hammer and Jack Man

By the light of a candle
the hammer man
wiped the sweat
from his brow
tightened his grip
shifted his weight
swung with faith.

Eight pounds of steel
stirred the dark
and hit the mark.
With a shattering crack
he hit the jack.

Steel on steel reveals
blessed sparks and
answered prayers.

The chisel man knelt
before the rock,
unfurled his fingers
and stole a breath.
Reset his grip
around the tip
and turned the jack
a quarter inch.

Day after day
life after life
men of flesh and bone
swung the hammer
turned the chisel
and beat the bloody
stone.

They set the pace
for an industrial race
built the guides
that shifted the tides
of war and peace
and turned history
a quarter inch.

Immigrant Miner

I flip through old pictures of miners
ponder the men of iron and gold
of copper and nickel, their thin
frail frames, their worn out shoes,
their wide brim hats and wet saggy clothes.

I see pictures of them marching
from the trenches to the mines
from concentration camps to mining camps
from digging in the soil to drilling in the rock.
A hoe in one hand and pick axe in the other.

Early millwrights built churches of
gold and coal, schools of silver and salt.
Blended philosophies like minerals
and welded clusters of cultures together.

Their history is one of slag and ash
and ground down gravel
shoveled up onto an iron horse
and spread out over the world.

The men in the pictures stare back at me
with the same curiosity I hold for them.
Their heads held high, their shoulders back
I feel the pride they hold in their slanted stances.
I want to superimpose myself alongside them
reach out and shake their callused hands.

The past and the present,
nature and industry, two
sides to the same coin.

Trapped

Every night when I was a boy
I'd huddle under the covers
where the air was stale and hot.

A flashlight for a head lamp
my feathered pillow, a forgiving
rock laid across my legs,
I'd pretend I was trapped
underground.

On my skin, I could feel the dirt
earned from the playground.
I savoured the unruly grit like hard candy.
I wanted to learn what it meant
to grow up and be a miner
like my father and his father.
I wanted to know what it's like
to spend half your life buried alive.

But fatigue bore down on me,
my eyelids like pounding hammers.
I'd fall asleep and slip from beneath
the burden of worldly expectations,
kick the sheets off my bed
and dream my way back to the light.

Timber Dogs

Back in the day the old guys
would tell the new guys
to keep watch for timber dogs,
the pack of wild dogs
they said lived underground
ran through the tunnels
attacked miners.

In truth, a timber dog
was a four inch spike
used to hold together
beams in a mine shaft.

I bet when the hammer
hit the spike it barked back
echoed through the mine
and scared the hell
out of the man on watch.

For some of the new guys
wild dogs would have been
a welcome sight
once they learned the size
of a shaft spider.

Calloused

I was told
whispered stories
about the kind of men who
woke to raw eggs
and whiskey for breakfast.

Calloused men who
went to work every day
to sleep off the night before,
thought nothing of women
and even less of children.

Tight fisted men who
unearthed pride from bitter insults
measured their manhood in empty bottles
grew to savour the sour taste of sulphur
and life in a dark empty hole.

I was told of miners
hardened men from long before;
whispered memories meant
to be kept buried deep
below the surface.

Sudbury Saturday Night

Back in the day, if you didn't have
a shovel in one hand and a drink in the other
you didn't get any respect.

After their shifts, many miners
felt they deserved a drink
and never went home.
Left their lunch pails like headstones
at the end of gravel driveways
and went straight to the taverns.

Where bartenders collected their cheques
and handed them a loaf of bologna.
The rest of their pay drenched in
a desperate race to drown in drink.

Men competed with each other
lifted kegs of beer above their heads
arm-wrestled their lives away
for some kind of status.

Once, I dug through the slag
on a Sudbury Saturday night, and
the bar was but a stain of beer and blood.

This burnished breed of nickel plated man
had nothing left to measure except the hole
where they sat rusting in the dark.

Son of Industry

I'm the spoke in your wheel
the ring on your finger
the long forgotten penny.

I'm the metal that held back
the oncoming truck.
The spoon that feeds the hungry.
The gear that turns
the time on your wrist.

I'm the barrel, the bullet and the bomb
the machine that eats the world.

I'm the needle, the scalpel,
the battery that beats a new heart.

I'm the copper wire, the computer chip
minerals connecting body and mind.

I'm a man, a woman, a miner.
I'm the son of industry.

Two Weeks and a Shovel

Every man I knew
worked in the mines.
Every man except my father's father.
I assumed he'd never had
the chance to swing a shovel.
When I asked why, everyone laughed
and went about their business.

After he passed, I overheard the story.
During the Great Depression he stood
with hundreds of other men outside
the gates of a mining hiring office.
The shift boss called out the number
of workers needed for that day
then pointed into the crowd.
For two weeks he was chosen
as one of the lucky ones.

On his last day the shift boss
whispered to my grandfather
if he wanted to be chosen again
my grandmother would
have to pay him a visit.

That proposition ended
my grandfather's career
but make no mistake
he was a miner.
He knew how to swing a shovel.
He nailed that bastard of a boss
across the head with one.

Sulphur Sunrises
(For Laura Foreshew)

My brother and I roll out of bed
into a morning sun that shimmers
like gold in a stream.

My mother, with sleep still in her eyes,
gets us ready for school.
On our way out the door, she hands us
each a clean rag to cover our mouths.

We stand at the top of the trail,
a crooked stone spine spackled
with minerals from a fallen angel.

The copper sky burns our eyes, below us
we see a yellow haze of sulphur so thick
we taste it on our teeth.

We run fast, dodging dead trees,
jumping from rock to rock through a
forest of discarded match sticks.

At school, kids complain of stomach aches,
headaches and burning throats.
My brother and I rinse off our rags in the fountain
then hang them to dry on the backs of our chairs
for the long walk home.

One Hundred and Forty-Five Pounds

To work underground in the mines
you didn't need an education
you just had to be a man
you had to be willing
and you had to be
one hundred and forty-five pounds.

Every morning my father would
eat a banana and drink a glass of water
repeat this six more times
then stand in line knees bent,
stomach boiling, bladder bursting,
just so he could make the weight.
When he returned home, jobless,
my mother would watch over him
as he vomited for hours.

Some men would secure mercury
in a rubber tube, slip this weight
where the sun don't shine
risk their lives, just so they could
get a job where the sun never
shines.

Five years after my father was hired
the rules changed, as they always do.
You needed to know a trade
women could be hired
and you didn't need to be
one hundred and forty-five pounds.

Six Men

Before the Superstack was completed
Mother Nature christened us. The tornado
tested our concrete, branchless tree.
Some say the stack swayed ten feet on either side.

Six men were at the top.
Six men in a bucket.
Six men on the edge of industry.

Three days before, in the dark
after the boss left, the lift operator
offered to take my father to the top.
He jumped at the chance of
going up instead of down.

When they reached the top
ropes whipping, bucket bouncing
wind howling, my dad said
he stared out across the city.
House lights like a miner's head lamps.
In the dark his world looked the same.

Six men survived that day.
Six men touched the ground.
Six men left their jobs.
Went home to their families.

Six men, and a city, changed forever.

Shiftwork

When my mother sent me downstairs
to wake my father for dinner, I'd stand
at the foot of his bed, the hot afternoon sun
dripping off me, his room dark and quiet,
the angles of his body rigid, even in his sleep.
He was a bear in a cave and I was
a curious boy with a stick.

I'd grab his toes, shake them,
yell "Dad," then pull back.
If I stood too close,
I'd be struck by his darkness,
knocked to the floor by a man
desperate for something to hold on to,
frightened of the dark hole beneath him.

He'd jump out of bed,
swing his arms and legs
as if he was trying to
catch himself mid-fall,
then he'd sit on the edge of his bed,
determined to find his bearings.
His mind digging for a safe place,
searching for something to ground him:
the day, the time, one of us.

I'd watch, as he'd
bolt himself back together
with grains of sand
and bright shards of light.

My mother said
his working shiftwork
kept him off balance.
She would tell us
he needed to reset his
soul with the sun.

Swatting Flies

My dad's voice was loud, his deep
tone rang through the neighbourhood
like a large dog chasing you down.
He worked in the mines where machines
were always running, and still ringing
in his ears when he was home.

He said sounds underground
bounced off the rocks
echoed through the tunnels
amplified his darkness.

One night, I lay in my bed
listening to him stomp around the house.
He was digging around for something,
then like a shifting fault in the earth
his voice bounced off the walls.

"Where the hell is the fuckin' flyswatter?"

I panicked and retraced my steps
my memory crumbling
behind closed eyes.

From the darkness roared a thunderous blast
then another and another, shaking the house.
I didn't feel safe until I heard a slap
from the flyswatter, then another and another.
I felt the sting, saw the red stain on the table
and pulled the covers up over my head.

In the morning, I found a twelve inch spike
driven into the wall. From it, the flyswatter hung.
A week later, he removed the spike
but the hole remained.

The hole always remained.

Precious Metals

A miner's affection is difficult to discover;
a soft word off a foul tongue
is a gem, hidden amongst casual phrases.
A rough hand to the top of your head
or a punch to the shoulder
is one hell of a find, if you know
what you're prospecting for.

When you do unearth an honest
gem of affection - like a favourite childhood
colour, sky blue - it hits you
with a rush, detonates your core,
leaves you smiling and panning
for more.

You can try to dig emotions out
of a hard rock miner, chip away
at their silence with a pickaxe,
blast through them with your heart,
but it won't do any good.

They're trained to safeguard against
a cave-in. They'll scoop up your fractured
mountain of emotions, and for safety reasons
crush them down to size.

Miners need time for their precious metals
to find their way to the surface.

In a world as refined as theirs
a simple nod of the head can say

I love you.

The Lunch Pail

Sitting right where you left it
waiting amongst our shoes
your lunch pail
all folded metal and rivets
cold to the touch, dented
and shiny.

Your name carved into metal
like markings in a cave.

What secrets this magic box must hold.
Like where you go.
Like what you do.

I slip my fingers through the handle
and it squeaks and clanks like the front gate.
I shouldn't be touching it.
I know I'm not allowed,
but the hard steel frame calls to me.

I put my thumbs to the latches
and push with all my might.
They snap back, cracking like falling rock
and my hands retreat to my chest.
"These damn things never work."
I hear you say these words
all the time.

I turn the lid over
to a sound like grinding gravel.

I slide my fingers along the rough edges
and flinch as a turned up
rivet catches the soft flesh.
I raise my finger to my mouth and
taste the iron in my blood.

In the box, an old paperback
white owl cigars
a jack knife
an apple.

I add my favourite marble
in the corner and try to close
the lid but the latches won't snap back.
"These damn things never work."
I hear myself say for the first time.

A Father's Lessons

(In Memory of Dick Kerr)

Every day, my mother and I
would stand on the porch
send my father off to work
her fingernails digging
into the wood grain of the railing
as her husband climbed into an old truck
weighted down with hardened men.

The kind who pound their fists
on the table when they speak,
offer you a beer when you're nine,
call you a sissy when you cry.

Before my father left,
he'd tousle my hair and say,
"When I get back,
I'll teach you to ride your bike,
or tie a hook to your fishing line,
maybe catch a fly ball, or how to talk to girls."
Then he'd wink and be on his way.

One day the truck never arrived
the men stayed home.
There was one less man to travel with
one less father making promises.

Alone in the backyard,
I tossed a ball into the empty blue sky
listened through an open window as
my father sat in the arms of my mother,
and cried.

Section II
Rite of Passage

Stone God

We walk into the earth
like we enter church on Sunday.
Bells replaced by sirens
hammers ringing hymns
hear our calling.

Our faith measured in blasted rock
our devotion proven in years of labour
we stand in line for our pay,
hands held out for the sacrament.

We kneel before our altar, a furnace,
and pray to the stone God.
He holds us in his iron cage of a fist
and drives us deep down into our faith.

We offer white smoke
rising from a concrete steeple
stacked as high as the heavens.

Now is the hour of sulphur and ash
of man and metal.

Blessed are those who
process ore in His name
for their work will
never be done.

Tremors

It's late and she can't sleep.
So she climbs out of bed
and thinks of him,
her other half, down
in a dark mine.

Her body is tired, but her thoughts
are trapped with him in
the centre of the earth.
She won't know if he's alive or dead
until the sun cracks the room open
until he holds her in his arms.

She paces the house, can't recall
if she let the cat in or not.
Stands with the door open
stares into the night
and calls for the cat.

He appears on the fence,
she takes the cat in her arms
her bare feet kissing
the cold earth through which
she senses her husband's heartbeat.
She can sleep now.

He's alive.

Men of Steel

(McIntyre Powder)

The sign hung on the front door:
in the change house
you should breathe deeply
and through your mouth.

We were young and naïve
eager to prove ourselves men
so we did what we were told
and didn't ask questions
because if we did
we'd be fired.

We'd march into the mines dry
and see rows of our work clothes
hanging on hooks, limp and dead
like a tainted meat locker.

We'd remove our street clothes
and whisper a silent prayer.

Without warning the doors closed
the ventilation shut down
every miner tightened up
with fear and held their breath.

In the change house
you should breathe deeply
and through your mouth.
Black powder filled the room
tiny aluminum particles
coated our lungs
like armour for our insides.

Some of us would tie a rag
over our mouth and face.
Others buried themselves
in their hands.

A few frightened men
stumbled about the room
desperate to swallow,
their hands at their chest.
Fear had found a crack
and it was digging in.

Small pieces of them
were being taken away.
They were being mined.

In the change house
you should breathe deeply
and through your mouth.

The Cage

Before we went up in the glass elevator
we stood with our faces to the sky
and stared up at the CN Tower.
My dad gave us each a stick of gum
to relieve the popping in our ears.
A young guide delivered a speech
about the speed of the elevator
and the height of the tower.
When she finished, my father laughed.

At the mine, he would go down into the earth
shoulder to shoulder with a dozen other men
in a tin can with half a gate for a door
and only a bell to ring to the man on the surface.

They called it the cage.
It smelled of grease, diesel, sweat and fear.
The walls rattled and shook as metal
scratched screaming at the rock.
Flashes of light flickered by as miners
passed the nine levels of hell.

The cage went down faster
and went deeper into the earth
than this marvel of a tower stood.

When we reached the top,
my father became quiet, held my hand,
as if the lights had turned on,
as if the city had become
the ceiling of the Sistine Chapel
and he had been touched by God.

Slag Dump

When I was a kid, my parents
packed us into the station wagon
and hauled us out to watch
the slag dump.

They stayed in the car
and steamed up the windows,
while we stood outside, felt the heat
from the red veins that
crawled down the hillside.

My uncle told me hot slag
could melt a body in seconds
not even the teeth remained.

People stole truck loads of it
to fill their driveways, until
they discovered toxins
leeched from it like pus from a wound.

The mines have since scribbled over the slag
with peat and lichens, and trees line the ridge.
Bee hives have been installed to soften the image
now honey crawls down the hill instead of slag.

Tailings Pond

They were fearless,
the three girls we met that night.
They said they were going swimming
so we followed, as boys do.
They pulled off the side of the highway
peeled back a section of chain link fence
and led us down a narrow path
to their secret swimming hole.
The pond was no more than a footprint,
surrounded by blasted rock and
trees no taller than we were.

Towering in the background
like a rogue wave, was the slag heap,
its shadow holding hands with the pond.
One by one the girls dove in and swam
along that thin edge of darkness, and
our eyes never left them as they
dipped in and out of the light.
Their fearless spirit as bright
as the stars some summer nights.

They asked us to join them
but we knew this was a tailings pond
the water pumped in from the smelter.
They laughed, told us
whatever was in the water
already swam through our veins.

Union Dues

A hunk of rusting metal in a puddle of mud.
This was our car, our driveway.
For nine months we received
thirty-five dollars a week because
the miners were on strike.

I stood barefoot in ripped jeans
on the hood of our broken-down symbol of freedom.
Watched as my dad and the neighbour - a big man
on compensation for back problems - moved
our washer and dryer over to his house.
Word on the street was the bank was
on the march to repossess.

At Christmas, we received a basket from the church
like our door had been marked with a red X.
Baskets dotted the streets.
My mother cried when she opened the door
and bankruptcy soon followed.

I'd sit in our broken-down car
turn the key to the engine over and over
as the car and I slowly rusted away.

When the strike was over, the union said
we had won, that things would be better
but all I saw for the next two years
was my dad walk down the back lane,
his shoulders a weighted scale,
lunch pail in one hand, groceries in the other.

Chiselled Out of Stone

At one time, this city
had a single plan
for every young man;
a straight, well-worn path
from their front doors
to an open rock face
at the end of a mine shaft.

A path chiselled out of stone,
a path paved in nickel.

Every young man wanted
his millwright ticket,
studied the ticking of gears,
the composition of rock;
had the culture of mining
drilled into him.

Plans were passed down
from lunch pail to lunch pail.
Fathers and sons dug the same holes
fought the same fights.

How many boys
has this rock hardened
into men.

Rite of Passage

When I turned sixteen, my feet
were the same size as my father's.
To him, that meant it was time for me
to become a part of the workforce.

One evening the family
gathered around the table
as my dad presented me with
a pair of new work boots
courtesy of the local mine.

The smell of leather filled the room
inflated me with pride.
My father, razor-blade in hand, sliced
the external guard off the boots
like he was removing foreskin.
This ritual revealed to the world
that I wasn't a miner.

I slipped the boots on,
felt taller, stronger, bolder.
I pulled the long laces tight,
wrapped them around the shaft
then tied them the same way
my father tied his boots.

In my tribe, the journey from boy to man
is taken in a pair of steel toed work boots.

Solid Ground

My first job was two hundred feet in the air
on the roof of a hoist room.
The boss, my grandfather,
lied about my age and told me
not to call him "Pépère"
but instead to call him
by his name, "Guy."

His words cut my life line
and left me off balance on this
forty by forty foot surface.
When the cage went up or down,
the absence of something solid
to hold on to shook me to my core
reminded me of my father
tossing me into my room.

I imagined my dad - a miner in the dark
below - falling away from me, reaching,
calling out my name.

It was strange to me, how my family
framed the outskirts of this city
like living bookends of earth and sky.

Smelter Dust

The dust that falls in a smelter
is overwhelming.

This dead skin of the earth doesn't
float in the air or glisten in the sunlight;
it falls grey and heavy seasoned with toxins.

An industrial ash that lines
the pockets of silent investors
coats their thin, oily comb-overs,
leaves a fingerprint on my history.

Try as I might, I can't seem to prevent
this sour residue from seeping out
from my pores and numbing my senses.
Generations of labour measured in
this lifeless sediment.

The dust that falls in the smelter
has choked out the world
and left me no choice
but to breathe it in and swallow.

Section III
Buffalo Souls

Buffalo Souls

This is the cold hard steel of it
the wheel and deal of it.
We're all cookie cutter kids
born in the shadow of the whale
sounds of production
ringing in our ears
and pupils dilated
to mushroom clouds.

We've been spit out
from the centre of the earth
shoved into graded lines
packed onto conveyer belt highways
bounced around and picked apart
designed and detailed by engineers
then pushed to our tensile strength.

We're kitchen sinks
and pocket change
rivers of sludge and slag
bullets and bearings
sulphur and smog
all circling the drain.

We're the hollow echo
of an industrial generation.
A plastic stir stick army
geared and numbered
displaced from nature and
balanced on the tipping point.
Re-manufactured buffalo souls
stampeding over the planet
and grazing on the future.

The Prospector
(Bjorkman Family)

The scar the axe left on her leg
is a Robert Service poem.
The pale crooked line
the first trail she ever cut.

A dying breed of aging men
with unkempt beards
told her she could never
be a prospector.

In the forest outside of
Whiskey Jack Lake
she sits alone on a rock
her skin burnt, bruised
and bitten, her hair a
tangled mess.

She wears her scare like a badge of honour
traces the jagged line with her finger
back to her home and recites
her favorite poem.

Industrial Cowboy

The old salesman had a knack
for remembering names.
A charm that resembled
the small gifts he'd come bearing
pens, flashlights, key chains,
any number of dollar store items.

A croupier tossing self-promotion
on our desks like poker chips.
He'd hypnotise us with
small talk. A snake-oil salesman
as charismatic as a shiny pair of new shoes.

Every move calculated,
every word rehearsed.
A math magician, a music man,
the violinist for a corporate orchestra.

He was like your favourite uncle.
He'd have you dancing down memory lane
and laughing from your stomach.
A game show host with the answers
hidden up his sleeve.

We'd watch him like a busker
on a street corner.
"You can't sell from an empty wagon,"
was his favourite line.

After his sales pitch,
I'd carry catalogues out to his car
which was soaked in saturated fats
and littered with the empty promises
of take-out containers.

Outside he'd light a cigarette
then lean in close, as if
he was about to tell you a secret.
Only to ask, "how long have you been working for?"
Then he'd flick his cigarette to the ground
and stub it out before you could answer.

He'd slump his shoulders, and
his eyes never left the ground.
He'd talk constantly, always
laughing at his own jokes.

On his way to his car
his feet only moved sideways
and his back was never
turned in your direction.

Before he'd leave
he'd slip you a sly smile,
nod, then stretch out his
sweaty hand to shake yours.

The old industrial cowboy
drove off into the sunset
and left us in his dust
primed and pumped to push
his product.

Cigarette Satellite

A miner stands in the darkness
his cigarette a satellite
dangling from his mouth
a beacon in the dark
for me to follow.

He leans in towards me
lifts my ear muff
and begins to yell,
"What you're hearing
is the sound of the drill
pounding into the rock.
It'll make you deaf."

Then he steps back,
takes a puff of his cigarette
and blows rings of smoke
out over his shoulder
not unlike the stack
on the surface.

Again, he leans in and
lifts my ear muff,
"What you're breathing
is a mixture of oil, gas, diesel
and a dozen other carcinogens,
I can't even begin to explain."

He takes a long drag
from his cigarette
then flicks it, and I watch
as my guiding light
disappears into the darkness.

This time he startles me
as he leans in,
"You're not allowed
to smoke down here,
smoking can kill you."

In the darkness I see
a milky-way of teeth appear.
Nobody's watching.
He's alone and he owns the dark.

In The Belly Of A Whale

The first time I met him was in the dark.
My light, shining upon his muddy face
made him look older than he was.
I was to spend a shift or two with him
learn from him, but
he barely spoke, and cast me aside.

I observed as he juggled his jackleg
water hoses and drill rods.
As he hammered at the darkness
harvested the rock face, laboured
like a giant squid in a dark ocean.

He was a shark circling me, so
my eyes never left him.
The sharpness of my stare
must have pierced his thick skin.
He set aside his jackleg,
turned around and considered me,
then waved me into
the deep end of the dark.

Without a word he taught me to drill
into the hard surface of a rock
read a stone's secrets, respect
this deep sea of darkness and
the Earth's jagged history.

In the belly of a whale
he signalled with his hands
pointed with his light and
taught me to read a man's eyes.

Masked Man

After thirty five years
they called him into the office
red faced and frustrated they screamed
their fingers hammering down on the table
pointing to a signature.
"Is this you?"

For years the miner had
signed his name this way
never quite understanding why.
Waiting for someone to notice.

The miner clenched his fists
and narrowed his steel eyes.
His armour could reveal
no cracks.

His superiors were ex-miners
they had experience in
unmasking the fault
in a hard rock face.

"What's the difference
in the name I sign? He said,
To you I am only a number."

Only after he left
did his bosses notice
high above the entrance
spray-painted on the rock face
in bright red letters
the same scribbled mark
from their papers.

"Zorro"

Millwright

He was a big man
well over six feet for sure
a millwright in a pair
of orange overalls
symmetrically covered
with strips of silver
reflective tape.

Two white bags, stuffed
with the tools of his trade
protrude from his back
like fractured wings.

A scuffed-up hardhat
large black ear muffs
on either side protected
his head, and gave him
the appearance of an insect.

He stood there alone
beside a red metal bin
brimming with broken
oily machine parts.

He was staring down
at his steel-toed boots
as they gently framed
a monarch butterfly.

"I need to protect it," he said.
As if it were a part of him
that had fallen off,
and he was at a loss
as to how to reattach it.
As if it were the last
beautiful thing on earth.

Rock Star

He strutted through the door
pulled off his Maple Leafs hat
tousled what was left of his hair
and stood at the front counter.
A sly grin on his thick-skinned face
his hands drum-rolling
the only tune he knows.

In this town he is a rock star
the top purchasing agent in a mining city
the man with his finger on the pulse.
With the stroke of a pen or the push of a button,
he could breathe life into a small business
or shut its doors forever.

The rumour was that at Christmas
cars hung around his block like gold chains.
Merchants lined up to kiss
his ring and his kitchen table overflowed
with bottles of liquor and gift cards
tickets to hockey games and trips to tropical places.
I once heard that someone even placed
a new snow machine at his altar.

When his hands stopped drumming,
our service counter went silent
and he sang his chorus
out of tune and off key.

"What do you got for me?"

I had nothing left to give
and I told him so.

The Meeting

The air was heavy and tasted like salt.
Our eyes hung like anchors on air balloons
and when someone said the word break
we lifted from our seats
like we were lighter than air
and sifted through the doorway.

Outside it stopped raining
and the summer air was fresh.
We stood in complete silence
breathed in the freedom.
The boss took out a cigarette
and flicked open his lighter.
Over and over again
his thumb hammered down
on the little wheel,
but he couldn't get a spark.

He shook the lighter and then
tapped it against his thigh,
blocked the wind with his hand,
hunched his back, contorted his
shoulders out of place,
then grinded the gears once more
but still no spark.

He returned the lighter to his pocket
and retrieved a musty pack of matches.
One by one, he tore them from the others
scratched their heads against
the rough surface of the pack
but still nothing.
They crumbled in his hands.

"They must have been in my pocket too long,
turned into duds" he said.
Then the door swung open.
One by one we filed into line
and funnelled back through
the hourglass door.
With a deep breath and a
sudden rush of stale heat,
we settled back into the meeting.

Company Men

Cautious of the terrain - like an animal
travelling from forest to field - I drive up
to the mine's main gate.

This place is a hive of activity;
the company's high resolution snow
records the miners' tracks.
Corporate records of
our comings and goings
like some kind of documentary
for the Discovery Channel.

The slanted morning light
distorts my world, or
so I tell myself every day
before I sign in and
leave my full name at the gate.

My identity replaced
by a corporate logo.
I am a cork board;
my employers pin tasks to me,
then wipe their hands clean.

I think of the old retired men
I see wandering about the city
looking for parts for a project
they say they are working on.

I know they're rummaging
through old hunting grounds
searching for pieces
of the name they were given
before they became
company men.

Shipper Receiver

I stand in a dimly lit warehouse
with one door and no windows
a lukewarm coffee for a friend
and a radio that's never quite on station.

I wait and watch as the day backs up
parks at my door and with an airbrake sigh
the morning delivers the world
one piece at a time.

I receive, and receive, and receive
plastic rumours and metal emotions
radio waves seasoned with opinions
life stories in fragments of shredded sentences
small styrofoam prayers dedicated to mothers.

I sign for it all, years of parents screaming
skids of IKEA instructions
bubble wrapped babies
envelopes of drunken philosophy
the bolted down cross my brother bears
all that the world has to offer.

I sort and organize this life
of unmarked dangerous goods
friendships and family, broken chess pieces
mislabelled angels, politicians made of shattered glass
and a mosaic of withering religions;
everything stacked together on numbered shelves.

I ship out the things I've learned,
packed and wrapped in newspaper
stuffed in recycled corrugated cardboard boxes
marked with red fragile stickers, prepaid and
labelled heavy with no return address.

In the end, I'm just a kid trying to throw rocks
in alphabetical order.

Section IV
The Taste of Sulphur

How to Lift and Carry a Load

Mounted on the wall before me
like it was carved in stone for Moses:
rules for lifting and carrying a load.

They read:
"Plan your lift. Ask yourself,
is the path ahead clear?"
How does a newborn babe
know the weight of its future?

"Ask for help."
Such easy instructions to write,
but hard to do, when
those around us are
overburdened with
their own fates.

"Get a firm footing."
In this department, I was lucky.
Born in a safe country, to a solid family.

"Bend your knees. Keep
the principles of leverage in mind."
Is my back the fulcrum of industry?
If you are not seen or heard,
do you have weight?

Now, "Tighten your stomach muscles."
I try to think of a time
when they weren't tight,
when my muscles weren't
held hostage, in knots.

"Lift with your legs."
The pillars of industry.
For heaven's sake,
don't let the ones at the top
do any lifting.

"Keep the load close."
It's yours now,
a box filled with your history,
every choice you ever made.
Handing this box off
is not an option.

Most important of all,
"Keep your back straight.
Move forward and don't twist."

I read the rules again,
and again, and again.
Search for the line that's missing.
The one we spend our lives
working towards.

The line that explains
how to set the load down.

Fruits of My Labour

The fruits of my labour grow
on assembly lines, not vines.
My hand-woven basket
is a corrugated cardboard
box.

The orchard I tend to
has rows of metal shelving.
The harvest I gather
is picked off of flat
smooth branches made
of cold hard steel.

The sun that shines down
is a yellow haze of halogen light.
The rain, dollar bills controlled
by a corporate irrigation system.

I look from my window
and see fields paved with cars
like fermenting produce
in a spoiled landscape.

I am a farmer of industry.
When you bite into the fruit
of my labour, oil drips
from your chin.

It won't ever ripen or bruise.
It won't rot or attract flies.
It's seedless, tasteless and
will never fill your belly.

My Calendar

They took down the art calendar
the only window with a view out of this warehouse
paintings of perfection and possibility
timeless snapshots from another world.

Instead, they've left me with a cold
hard numbered year devoid of emotion
all steel precision and math
a worthless flap of dead skin
hanging off the wall.

A scab that begs to be picked at
peeled off and tossed.

There is nothing here
to pry open my mind's eye
to peek at who I might have been.

Where will I go to hide
when the snakes come slithering in
when the ants go marching by
when the bear charges, and
the lion roars?

I want to slice my finger
and smear blood on the wall
where my calendar should be
but they wouldn't understand.

Instead, I will fade
and leave no stamp on the world.
Crumpled up like a wasted piece of paper
like this memo about calendars, and
my life, lost in a mountain of blank days.

Scrap Metal

In the scrapyard
men in birdlike masks
breathe fire, chew up steel
into bite sized pieces
and from their junkyard nest
regurgitate metal into
our open mouths.

An elephant of a machine
moans in pain, stomps and crawls
its way across this
rust coloured jungle.
A magnet on chains sways through
the oxidized air like a trunk.

The lodestone picks up
old washers and dryers,
boats and motors, cars and trucks,
stacks them into jagged steel mountains.

I watch as a rhino of a bulldozer
buries the elephant's scraps,
instinctively returning
the metal to the earth.

From where I stand,
I can see the smokestack
the dragon's throat
as it huffs and puffs
and devours raw ore.
I open the trunk of my car
empty the metal body parts
scrap metal reciting poetry.

Zero Harm

Before a shift starts
men gather in a misshaped circle
and the shift boss informs them
zero harm is the goal.

Zero harm in our kitchens, in our schools
and in countries with names we can't pronounce.

Zero harm to the planet we rape and plunder
to the neighbour we covet, and in the breath we exhale.

Zero harm in the backseat of our fathers' cars
and in the promises we whisper to each other.

The shift boss talks about safety from
a safe distance, as miners slip under the earth
in their shells, black and hard as the backs of beetles.

Rocks fall with the earth's every breath.
Men of the deep pray to the sun
and listen for the bells of faith
to ring them home.

I once met a man from mine rescue.
He investigated accidents underground,
reconstructed a miner's worst fear,
then advised on how to
zero the harm from every action.

He said to me, "When the goal is clear
and we're focused, we are at our finest
and our most vulnerable."
Every day the men gather in a misshaped circle.
The boss informs them that zero harm is the goal.

My knees buckle from the weight of his words.

Scabs

Banners waving, miners on the march.
"Our lungs are full of Nickel!
And our hearts are full of pride!
If you're a scab!
You got nowhere left to hide!"

A friend of mine, a carpenter,
told me he was out of work.
He refused to cross the picket line.
His dad had worked for INCO for thirty years.

I wondered, if my work were to ask me
would I do the same, refuse?
It makes no difference now.
I've been laid off.

I step outside, look across the street,
see some men shingling the roof.
Maybe I could go back to
the rooftops of the city?

I read the sign on the truck:
"Miners on Roofs".
One of the guys walks towards me:
"Hey, want to support some miners on strike?
We'll do your roof, cheap."

I know him, went to school with him;
brand new house, just built.
Two boats, four-wheelers, a camp,
and a big ass truck to go with it all.

I look at my car rusting in the driveway,
wonder where I will get this week's payment.
I don't answer him, just stare
then walk back into the house.

In this city, we have all been cut
deep, and every four years
we go pick at the scabs.

Blowing in the Wind

I was never taught to read the wind
never learned to streamline my thoughts
so I could attain less resistance
from a real estate agent,
never understood the
energy content of a breeze,
and certainly never considered
buying a house
in the basket of an air balloon.

I did, however, read the book
Who Has Seen The Wind
It offered no insight to the
purchase of a new home.
Nor did the author describe carcinogens
that ride on the breeze like Hell's Angels.

So when my friend informed me
he bought a house because the smoke
from the stack rarely blew in this direction,
it knocked the wind out of me.

I wondered if my brick house
was merely a straw house
in wolf's clothing.

Clean Shaven

The request was simple,
sounded legitimate,
and it was for safety.

"Anyone entering onto mine property
must be clean shaven.
There must be a perfect seal
between your mask and your face."
Like the way an old black and white
photo is sealed in an album.

I held the razor to my face,
could feel the company's thumb
pushing down, and watched
as tiny black follicles of identity
fell into the white bathroom sink.

When I finished, my daughter
pushed me away, started to cry.
I retrieved our photo albums,
pointed out some pictures of me,
clean shaven,
but she pushed them away,
pushed me away, told me
I wasn't her daddy.

Strike Mandate

I sit on a park bench, newspaper in hand
watching as my son enters
the playground, shy, and cautious.

He doesn't know these kids.
No rules have been established.
No boundaries have been drawn.
There is no rank set in this park.

I think nothing of it,
begin to read the paper.
The local miners have been on strike
out for over two months now.
Egos flaring, tempers sizzling
on the pavement outside the gates.

The front page story reads,
"Vale employee assaulted while jogging."

I look up from my paper,
check on my boy.
He is sitting, playing
with a pile of rocks.

Two boys circle him, try to
pull him away from his claim
but he stands his ground.

One of the boys runs off
while the other stays and plays.

Negotiations

We mince each other's words with
shredded letters and mislaid memos.
Fine print chips our teeth
and leaves us pacing the floor
with a double-edged tongue.

We thrash our arms about
inflate and pound our chests
throw rocks at each other
from the ends of our driveways.

Until our hands blister
and we take our eyes out.
Until our streets sizzle
with backroom deals.
Until the taste of sulphur
no longer registers
and the only meal served
at any table is compromise.

Only then will we amend
our phrasing, haggle with
the gate keeper, shift our weight
and dance with a third-party.

Only then will we reveal
our hands with open palms
and bargain for our livelihoods,
our promises adding up like
slanted stacks of coins.

In the end, we'll burn
our pride in a barrel,
lock our conscience
in a desk drawer, chew
on our choices until
they curdle in our stomachs.

In the end we'll give birth
to a new contract
and these negotiations
will be nothing more
than forgotten labour pains.

Level Three Alarm

At six am, an air horn rang out.
Turn off your intake systems, close
all windows, keep your doors shut.
A hornet's nest had been kicked.
Emergency measures have been activated,
level three emergency, traffic shut down
for miles around in all directions.

Miners flew out of the smelter, masks on
buzzed about the grounds as a yellow plume
of nitrogen dioxide and monoxide hung above.
An industrial acid plant spewed its pollen
spread its seed to our lungs, throats, eyes and skin.
A toxic shadow that irritated
everyone who lives in this city
in one way or another.

By the time I drove to work
the queen bee had told us she was satisfied.
Due to wind speeds and weather conditions
the mist had cleared, and the community was deemed safe.
The sirens ceased, and traffic started to flow.
I looked up at the stack, and turned on the air
conditioning, breathed, and tried to reassure myself.
At least these mines aren't nuclear plants.

Labour Temple

The President of the Steelworkers said,
"Next to losing a family member,
this is the most traumatic event in my life."

The Mayor was quoted as saying,
"All my victories were celebrated
in that hall and all my defeats."
He called the building a "labour temple."

The Steelworker's Hall
is the working man's university
home to callused hands, sore
backs, and widows.

Early one morning, the hall
burned down, silenced
by the ignorant embers
of two young boys.

Excavators pulled
apart the walls like shaking
hands disengaging.

People gathered in crowds
mourned and watched as smoke
rose into the sky alongside
the smoke from the stack.

Fool's Gold

I have witnessed men stand
at a crossroads of tunnels,
trade the minerals in their soul
for a handful of rocks.
Watched as their lungs filled with
chemicals and their hearts turned to slag.

I have dragged men through
the dark halls of the earth
as their shadows clawed at
jagged rocks. Whispers
from demons calling on a debt
no honest man could pay.

Men who have spent their lives
sick to the rhythm of the earth.
I have found these men with clenched fists
curled up at the end of a hollow shaft
crying out in the dark
screaming in pain for the light
begging the dirt for redemption.

In the end they took their pay
filled their pockets with paper bills
and buried their pain on the ride home.
Their mouths packed with crushed dirt
and primed to burst with jagged teeth.

Men, brittle boned and shallow skinned
eyes brushed with the dust of fool's gold.
Their pupils a dark pit, their fingers
pried open by loved ones.

They've spent their last days
on their knees in the rubble
of crushed homes
staring into empty palms.

Man Of Minerals

The old man scoured the streets
for scrap metal like a stray dog
sniffing around for his home.
When he found a promising piece
he would hold it up close
touch it to his face.

If he suspected it was copper
he would put it to his lips
breathe in deep through his nose
and wait for the image of a baby.

Lead he bent and twisted in his hands
tried to coax an image out of the mineral
tried to pry a picture of his boys fishing
from the metal's clenched fist.

Stainless steel he would cast aside.
He knew in an instant it was a decoy
a distraction to the soul
not to be trusted.

Brass he would spit on and shine with
the sleeve of his wool sweater
run his fingers across the surface
as if reading memories in braille.

If you placed a nickel in his palm
he would clasp his hands together and pray
then cry like a child who lost its mother.

He's no longer around, the metals of his body
returned to the soil from which they came.
He had spent the end of his life prospecting
the streets for the three sons he lost to the mines.

Mining Town

When the drills fall silent
when the hammering stops
when sirens sing their warning song
this city holds a single breath.

We all lean in together
brace for the blast and
hold on for the aftershock.
A star has exploded.
A rock has fallen.

A miner has died.

We fall through a list of names
and cut ourselves on every syllable.
Fathers, uncles, siblings, friends
crumble into rubble
like sand through our fingers.

We call the ones we love
but their ears are stone walls.
Their mouths a hollow shaft that echoes
our own crushing thoughts.

We want a name, one we don't recognize.
We want a place, one we're not a part of.
We want to reach down into the earth
and pull our roots out from this rock
but it's too late.
A miner has died.

We all lean in together
stare into the empty hole and scream.
I knew them. I miss them. I loved them.
Only silence echoes back.

Blasting Hour

I dream of surfing a wave
of black slag – the one I see from
the back door of my apartment.
I ride the groundswell to the shore
of some big city – not this one - escaping
the big bully smokestack as it screams
out foghorn obscenities and tries to choke
out all my ambition.

For so long, I have felt
like a ship without a captain,
an empty vessel pounding against
the rocks, time washing me away
like water over stone.

Only the blasting hour remains
that moment every night
when the men of the deep
blast the rock under my feet
shake the covers off my bed
and throw stones at me.

Minerals wash up against
the back of my eyelids,
grinding out demands.
"What do you want, boy?
Are you going to sink or swim?"

I tell myself, tomorrow
I will stop treading water,
start swimming lessons, build
a life boat.
I tell myself, tomorrow I will
be ready for the blast.
But I never am.

The Taste of Sulphur

The sour taste of sulphur
reminds him of who he is
when he drinks too much rye.
A flavour that sends him
staring into the mirror, digging
deep into his reflection.

On these mornings, when
the air is thick and yellow
and he can't seem to drag himself
to the surface and go to work,
the dryness in his mouth prevails,
overloads his senses, and crushes him
with the acid fallout of a mining town.

Every malicious word, every spiteful action,
every day wasted feeding the beast
is unearthed as a pin hole, a
rust spot on the surface of his soul.

Slag decisions of arsenic and lead
seep through his pores and
poison those around him.
Self-inflicted scars by the shovel full
by the bottle full, by the generation
cave in around him.

The company offers to help,
gets him a professional to
bury the debris, pick at the vein
until it bleeds, then they cover up
the scars with a new paint job
but this only lasts a couple of years.

The rust still lies below the surface,
scratching at his subconscious. The
sulphur still burns his lungs yet day
after day he keeps digging.

Section V
Slagflower

She Becomes the Light

Unlike the men, before every shift,
she did her pre-check, flicked every switch
kicked every tire, inspected every inch
of her equipment, as if she were gazing
into her lover's eyes, probing for lies,
sniffing the air for an unfamiliar scent,
listening for a loose word.

She wasn't your run of the mill miner
she wouldn't push herself or
her machine too far.
If something was out of place or
damaged, she'd call the hazard in
and have the defective part replaced.

She understood that if you
neglected a blinking light, or
disregarded a small crack and
turned a blind eye to the rock
people died.

She was shown the lay of the land
the hard way, from hard men.
Their open pit mouths gave her
nothing but rude remarks
and their blistered hands offered
nothing but filthy gestures.
Behind her back, even her boss
would brand her bad luck.
When she walked on the jobsite
men walked off the job.

Deep underground in a man's world
she sparked against the rough edge
of industry yet still carried
the same weight as any other miner.

Even when her surface was crushed to dust
and the days lost their meaning
and the sun stopped rising in her eyes
she held her head up and
stayed faithful to herself.
In a dark place, during a dark time
she became the light.

Converter Aisle

Standing by the converter aisle
where rock is smelted into metals.
I was waiting for my contact person
and doing what someone does
in a strange place.
I was checking it out.

What caught my eye
was a worn out poster
of a woman in a bikini.
Most of the picture
had been scraped off the wall.
Only her face and
part of her shoulder remained,
stonewashed and faded.

I was able to date the photo
from her long feathered bangs
and big hooped earrings.
She must have been
a model in the seventies.

Branded into the brick beside her
were three other blank spaces
with the same measurements.

I began to notice
these missing women everywhere
beside the phone, on the wall
where a calendar once hung
in the bathroom stalls
on lockers and lunch pails.
I even saw the outline of a sticker
that resembled a pin-up girl, on a forklift.

When my contact arrived,
there was a student with him.
She was young, and tall,
with long blonde hair.
I did my best not to stare, not to
fill in the blank spaces with her image.

Rock Cuts

The gateway to this city
is lined with blasted rock
a highway that stretches out
like exposed bone, revealing
our fractured path to this place.

The road's edges framed by
the hardened flesh of the earth
the peeled back skin of rock.

This is a city of mines
of multiple stab wounds,
of severed arteries that emit
the stench of sulphur, bleeding
ore.

To stop the infection
we cauterized the earth
and blackened a layer of skin.
To help us breathe
we inserted a concrete scope
into the city's throat.

We put this place on life support.
We dress the cuts with grass and moss
and plant a thousand trees a year.

There are no signs, no maps,
no head lamps to lead the way.
But if any place can navigate
the pot-holes on this highway
and be a light for the world to follow
through this industrial tunnel
it's this city.

Thirty Years in the Hole

In line at the local watering hole
waiting for my morning coffee
a group of retired muckmen
sit in the corner like
a bask of crocodiles.

One is chomping on the bit
grumbling about how the government
spends seventy thousand a year
to keep a man in jail.
"They get free cable, an education,
time in the sun. What the fuck?"

Another says,
"Put them in the ground,
give me the money.
I never killed anyone."

Their hammering talk
starts to barrel roll.
"They would only need one guard.
There's only one way in, one way out."
"It's simple, if they don't work,
they don't eat."
"Turn off the lights, the air,
the work will get done."

They laugh, pat each other on the back
their bellies bloated with sugar-coated
cream-filled answers.
Their words like crumbs
litter the floor around me.

Every day it's the same.
Even after thirty years in the hole
these miners gather together
to kick the muck from their boots.

I pick at their chatter
like a small Egyptian plover
and my morning's oasis contracts.
The walls move in like closing jaws
and the line shuffles forward.

Inventory

I stand in the smelter warehouse
before rows and rows of old machine parts
bearings, belts, seals, and couplings that
no longer connect anything together.

I'm here to identify the inventory
clean, label, and catalogue.
To determine if there's anything of value
among these outdated, forgotten parts.

I put on my gloves, glasses, and mask.
God only knows the history
of the toxins lurking in this dust.
I think of Darwin on his islands
trying to classify the order of evolution.

At the end of the day, I'm shrouded
in the lifeless grime of industry.
Shadows of the parts I removed
dot the shelves like footprints in the snow.

I wonder if my father, or his father
worked with anyone of these same parts
pulled its brother or sister from the shelf
or perhaps placed a part here
for me to pick up and carry forward.

Full Circle

Two months after retiring from
years of working underground
the old miner went for
open heart surgery.

His body quaked and quivered
at the thought of his bare flesh
on a cold metal table. At the thought
of a stainless steel scalpel
kissing the minerals in his blood
like long lost relatives at the airport.

The thought of doctors
cracking open his ribs
digging in with both hands
following his veins to his heart.

The surgeon assured him
the procedure had advanced.
A remote controlled machine
would drill a small shaft
straight to the source
blow up one of his veins and
allow the minerals in his blood,
his fear, and his life's work
to come full circle.

Miner's Grave

Every day above ground
is a good day.

When I die, don't bother with
the fuss and muss of a fancy pine box.

Dig a hole and toss me in.

The earth should encompass my body
as it did the spade of my shovel.

I want my mouth to fill with dirt
so I can taste the deeds I have done.

I want the dirt to return the favour
and break apart my bones.

So my body will feed the earth
as the earth fed me.

If not, cremate me, shove me into
the furnace I fed for so many years.

Let my remains drift up the stack
and my ashes rain upon your gardens.

Better yet, leave me in the place
where the world has fallen in around me.

Stick a shovel in the ground above
and paint my name and these words upon it:

"We all dig our own holes."

God's Clenched Fist

Long white coats appeared
out of the dark like ghosts
so clean and pure
so out of place
2000 feet underground.

I always told myself that
if I became turned around or lost
I would follow the water
up and out to the surface.

These scientists were following the water
down, to the origins of life.
What they discovered were droplets
millions of years old, trapped
in God's clenched fist.

I watched the white coats
float past my drift like angels.
I slipped my glove off
touched the rock face
felt the water like
tears on my palm.

Miner Poets

I am at my parents' place asking
to borrow my dad's old metal lunch pail.
He tells me he tossed the damn thing
into the crusher on his last day of work.
A sacrificial offering some men make.
He said he didn't want to have anything
at home that reminded him of that place.

I remember tossing my books
over a bridge into a river
on my last day of high school.
The instant regret I felt as I watched
four years float down the river.
I couldn't imagine thirty years crushed.

We head down the street to my uncle's place.
He tells me he still has his lunch pail,
but I might not want it.
I hold the metal box in my hand.
My uncle spent thirty years underground
with a loon, on a blue lake, under a blue sky,
painted on his lunch pail.

I offer to set the pail free. Tell them,
"I want to use the lunch pail to carry my poems."
Confused, the two brothers look at me.
"Poetry? Where the hell do you get that from?"

Kitchen Sink

I don't remember my dad
ever doing the dishes
the chore was always left
for my sister and I.
The two of us would spend hours
talking, laughing, with our hands
in the kitchen sink, wet with life.

The issue wasn't that my dad believed
dishwashing was women's work
or that he was above such menial jobs.
He just didn't like the sink.

He said he knew where the damn thing came from
that most of the nickel he dug out of the ground
was formed into stainless steel kitchen sinks.
He saw his reflection in the steel.

I have my own house now and the sink
is made of some new age plastic.
I don't think this is better in any way,
but when my dad comes over for dinner
the two of us can spend hours doing the dishes.

Stepping Stones
(For Stephanie)

On the seventh day
God was skipping stones
across the universe and
one landed in our back yard.
My daughter picked it up and placed
the misshapen, stone heart into her
tiny hands.

She leaned in close and whispered
the secret wishes of a child.
She is teaching me
how to speak with the earth
how to decipher the art of nature.
For her, minerals are memories
every stone tells a story
every rock speaks poetry.

Words unearthed from the
driveways of friends and family
from hiking paths and riverbeds
souls picked from the soil
and named by a child.

In her room she piles them
in the shape of a grave
invites each stone to whisper
its secrets while she plays
hovering above like an angel.
So, this is heaven.

If she could, she would pick
the moon from the sky
and slip it into her pocket
and I would let her.

Smoke Signals

A month after I was born
the Superstack was completed
and ever since the smoke
has clouded my sky
loomed over me like a symbol
of strength and power
an industrial totem pole.

As a child my siblings and I
believed the stack puffed out
a long white streamer of clouds
like the rings my father made
with the smoke from his cigar.

We'd sit and watch from our
car window as this concrete lighthouse
sent out a beacon of smoke signals
that reached out for miles
seeped into our souls
and named each one of us.

These days when I drive home
my own kids look out the window
and search for a symbol of home.
I smile, as they yell in unison.

"Animal Bridge!"

Footprints

On top of Blueberry Hill
I shovel a handful of berries
into my mouth and look out across
the city's landscape.

Green leaves adrift on an ocean of rock
coloured shingles hidden in the swells
people thriving in the wake of industry.
It wasn't always this way.

In the early seventies astronauts trained here
came to see what we were geologically made of
and inadvertently left their footprints
on the backs of our miners.

Rumours grew like moss on stone
and the world likened us to the moon.
People said nothing could ever grow here
but I grew here and so did these berries
these tiny blue moons, these sweet tears of the sky.

I pick another one of these pale blue dots
place it in the universe of my hand
and consider all we have done.

I pop the world into my mouth
taste the history of our hard labour.
We've left our footprints
on the moon and beyond.

Rock Garden

We turn on to the off ramp
and on to the bypass, my toddler son
and pregnant wife by my side.
The back of our mini-van ripe
with empty pails that roll back and forth.

We park on the side of the highway and
I pick up a whittled slice of blasted rock
hold it to the sky, inspect it, as if
this cut stone was the key
to an ancient language.

I wave and point, like a cave man
then place the primal text in the bucket.
My wife and son pay no attention.
They are inspecting flowers
that have grown between the cracks
of these disfigured puzzle pieces.

On the way home we stop at the farmers' market.
The mines are giving away jack pine saplings
grown in a greenhouse deep underground.

I spend the remainder of my afternoon
with my hands in the soil of our backyard
arranging shredded rock into spiral writing
like a love letter to the earth.

When I finish, I call to my wife and son
and together, we plant the jack pine
in the centre as a peace offering.

This tree's branches will have a family
to help it fight for the light.

I look up from a hard day's work
my back stiff and sore
see the rocky hills that circle this city
and ripple out to the rest of the world.

When I was a boy
I played upon those barren rocks.
Back then, the tress were few and far
between, but now they fill in the cracks,
stretch towards the light and paint the landscape.

In the midst of a boreal forest,
this city is a rock garden.

Slagflower

Our fathers who came before us
men from many nations
braved the task of altering
stone to seed.

Their nickel-plated pollen
was hauled to the surface
and scattered about to form
pockets of change, the start
to an industrial revolution.

We were harvested from the minerals
of their calloused hands, planted
in the long shadow of our fathers' slag
raised to the common core of a mining town
then smelted into a life of iron and ore.

We have been milled in metaphor
and left rusting in the rain, but together
we've sprouted upon this rock
into a new shade of green
with sulphur-speckled leaves
and a sky-scraping stem
we bend to the light
and beg to bloom.

Acknowledgements

I would like to thank my wife Lisette for giving me the space I needed to write this book. We have a busy, beautiful life and yet you always made sure I had time for me.

My kids, Evan and Stephanie, for your support, love and understanding when I had to leave for writing events and for also giving me time and space to write. I couldn't ask for two better children.

My parents, Louis and Joan, the two of you molded me into the man I am today. Your unconditional love and support is the secret poem that binds this book together. Thank you so much.

My siblings and aunts and uncles, some of these poems are a part of you as much as they are a part of me. This book wouldn't be whole without you and neither would I. Thank you for your advice and support.

All the people involved in helping realize I am a poet and helping put this book together. Roger and Chris Nash for your mentorship and guidance. What the two of you have done for me, and all the writers of this city, will not be forgotten. Chris, your first draft helped me start to see the bigger picture of what I was doing. Irene Golas and Vera Constantineau (my writing wife) the two of you have taught me so much about poetry. You are always there for me. You made me a better writer and a better person.

The Sudbury Writers' Guild and the City of Greater Sudbury Public Library's Open Mic Night, attending these monthly events and meeting some incredible people and artists have inspired me and pushed me to be my best.

To my publisher, Latitude 46 Publishing, Heather Campbell and Laura Stradiotto, the two of you believed in this project before I think I did. I know it wasn't easy, but the two of you stuck with me and all my crazy ideas and you made it happen. I respect the hard work and dedication you both put into everything you do. You both work hard to make this city a better place to live, and I am proud to be a part of what you're accomplishing.

Kim Fahner and Daniel Aubin, the two of you both put your stamp on these poems. Kim, your sweet and honest edits helped me push my writing and understand the power of STANZAS. You were so right. Dan, your final edits and advice helped me put this collection into focus. Thank you for your time and your honesty.

And a big thanks to the City of Greater Sudbury and all of you who live here. You have inspired me, and raised me, and are a part of me. These poems are as much yours as they are mine.

About the Author

Thomas L. Leduc is the descendant of four generations of miners and works at an industrial supply company in Sudbury. His poetry and writing has appeared in anthologies and magazines in Canada and the U.S.. Thomas was Poet Laureate of the City of Greater Sudbury between 2014 and 2016. He is President of the Sudbury Writers' Guild. He lives in Sudbury with his wife and two children.